Road Transport Recollections
The Best of British

Paul Stratford

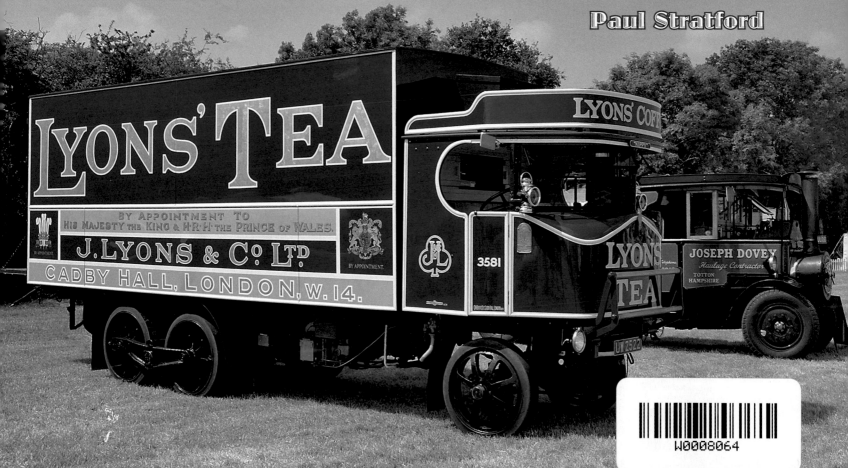

First published in 2019

British Library Cataloguing in Publication Data
A catalogue record for this book is available from the British Library.

ISBN 978 1 85794 552 2

Silver Link Publishing Ltd
The Trundle
Ringstead Road
Great Addington
Kettering
Northants
NN14 4BW

Tel/Fax: 01536 330588
email: silverlinkpublishing@btconnect.com.

Website: www.nostalgiacollection.com

Printed and bound in the Czech Republic

Title page: **Sentinel** 1929-built DG6 No 7966 is fitted with a stunning recreation of a box van body of a Lyons' Tea fleet vehicle.

Contents

Introduction

Prior to the 1840s large-scale stationary steam engines had been used in industry for driving heavy machinery in factories for a number of years, but it was not until the coming of the small portable engine, often moved around by a team of horses, that farms and smaller workshops were able to capitalise on steam power. It was not long before the self-moving steerable steam engine was introduced, probably credited to Rochester engineer Thomas Aveling, whose later steam roller products were known worldwide. The steam roller soon became an essential part in upgrading the cart tracks of the time to smooth and durable roads.

Not only were traction engines used as a power source for machinery, but with the improvement in the quality of the roads they were also used for hauling goods on heavily laden trailers across the country at a much quicker rate than the horses they replaced. The traction engine became an essential part of farm life, able to drive machinery, in particular threshing machines, then move the equipment on to another site. Supplied in pairs with a winching drum mounted beneath the boiler, the steam ploughing engine revolutionised ploughing and cultivation of arable farmland. With an engine situated at each end of the field, a large reversible plough would be winched back and forth, eliminating the single-furrow horse plough at a stroke.

The travelling fair, an important part of the social calendar, was soon to become an important customer for some manufacturers; the highly ornate showman's engine with its belt-driven dynamo could not only generate power for the rides and lighting, but could also haul the rides and equipment from town to town. One of the earliest customers, Anderton & Rowlands, still exists today, and while no longer using showman's engines, a number of the company's former engines survive in preservation.

The large road locomotive, while having the haulage capacity, lacked the flexibility that a wagon could offer. Foden and Sentinel were the major producers of steam wagons and tractors, but were not alone, with examples from other manufacturers surviving into preservation.

Great Britain was the foremost manufacturer and supplier of steam traction engines, both for the home market and worldwide, and it is a credit to the builders and the quality of the craftsmen that first, so many have survived, and second, that there are so many owners who have restored and maintained these engines as 'the Best of British' for everyone to enjoy.

Paul Stratford

Portable engines

Barrows of Banbury No 316 is one of the oldest surviving examples of a portable engine, circa 1870.

Farmers Foundry 1910-built 7nhp portable engine No 36, one of only two surviving examples, simmers away in a quiet corner at Old Warden.

Brown & May This diminutive 1868-built portable engine would have traditionally been moved around using horse power. Note how the chimney has been folded down to improve stability.

Merryweather No 1541, built in 1890, is not so much a portable engine as a horse-drawn portable steam fire pump, formerly from the Blenheim Palace Estate in Oxfordshire.

Road rollers

Aveling & Porter The iconic steam roller, this 10-ton example, No 9128 built in 1920, sports the 'Prancing Horse' emblem and 'Invicta' motto on the headstock, and looks at home in the contractor's yard in Astwood Bank.

Fowler DNB compound 10-ton roller No 17492, built in 1928, is fitted with tar-spraying equipment.

Aveling-Barford was one of the last manufacturers of steam rollers, and seen here in the Warwickshire village of Armscote is a 6-ton example, No AC 624 built in 1938.

Marshall Piston-valve compound 8-ton roller No 76116 *Maid Marion*, built in 1923, was photographed while attending an event in Moira.

Traction engines

Marshall No 37690 *Old Timer* is the engine owned by Arthur Napper that claimed victory in the famous 'Race for a Firkin of Ale' at Appleford in 1950.

Burrell Traction engine No 1127 *Lord Burrell*, built in 1884, is the fourth oldest surviving engine from this manufacturer.

Above left: **Savage** General-purpose engine No 474 is the sole survivor from this manufacturer. Built in 1889, it is seen at the Bloxham Rally.

Above **McLaren** No 551 *Centaur* was built in 1894, as is seen attending the Aston-on-Clun village festival.

Left: **Burrell** This company built its last road locomotive, No 4093 *Dorothy*, in 1931, and it is seen passing a typical Warwickshire thatched cottage.

Right: **Clayton & Shuttleworth** No 46059, with a female crew, passes through Weaverham in Cheshire on an organised Road Run Event.

Below: **Fowler** Road Locomotive No 12906 *Foremost* passes through the streets of the North Wales seaside town of Llandudno.

Below right: **McLaren** Road Locomotive No 1295 was repatriated after a working life in Argentina, and is seen here on an end-of-season outing in Worcestershire.

Above: **Marshall** Compound tractor No 78953, converted from a road roller, scurries along the A5 at Pentrefoelasin in North Wales.

Above right: **Robey** Traction engine No 28094, built in Lincoln in 1908, is a rare survivor and is proudly displayed at the Bloxham Rally.

Right: **Aveling & Porter** LC8 Colonial Road Locomotive No 5192, built in 1903, was repatriated from Mozambique and, now fully restored, is seen here at the Great Dorset Steam Fair.

Left: **McLaren**
Compound traction
engine No 1534, built in
1917, makes light work
of climbing 'Engine Hill'
from Porthtowan in
Cornwall.

Right: **Clayton &
Shuttleworth** No
44103 *Enterprise*, built
in 1911, passes through
Salford Priors in
Warwickshire.

Above: **Wallis & Steevens** Traction engine No 2394, converted from a road roller, climbs up into the village of Acton Bridge in Cheshire on one of the hottest days of the year.

Right: **Fowler** Road Locomotive No 13141 *Jo* is visiting the Crich Tramway Museum in Derbyshire.

Above: **Aveling & Porter** No 8401 *Avelina*, a compound traction engine, heads for Anglesey along the A5 in Wales.

Right: **Tasker** Compound traction engine No 1709. built in 1916, attends a rally held at Fawley Hill, home of the late Sir William McAlpine.

Right: **Marshall** No 17134 *Mary Margaret* was declared the winner of the Wirksworth Assessment Trials held in Derbyshire in 2014.

Below: **Burrell** Double-crank compound No 4019, built in 1925, was photographed while attending a National Traction Engine Trust Driving Weekend at Astwood Bank.

Opposite: **Mann** 4nhp tractor No 1325 *Myfanwy*, seen at Onslow Park in Shropshire, has an unusual rack-and-pinion steering arrangement.

Above: **Burrell** Road Locomotive No 3941 *The Badger*, resplendent in crimson lake paintwork, heads through the village of Offchurch in Warwickshire.

Left: **Fowell** Traction engine No 108, one of only seven survivors from this Huntingdonshire manufacturer, is seen at the Great Dorset Steam Fair.

Opposite: **Garrett** 4CD tractor No 33278 *Princess Mary* is seen in a typical rural farmyard setting.

Fowler No 19456 *Highland Lass*, a compound tractor rebuilt from a roller, graces the charming setting of Lower Slaughter in the Cotswolds.

Right: **McLaren** No 1242, a traction engine built in 1911, was exported to New Zealand, but returned to the UK briefly in 2010 and is seen here at Old Warden.

Below: **Foster**, or more specifically William Foster & Co of Lincoln, built No 14593 in 1927. It was once owned by the Reverend Teddy Boston, rector of Cadeby in Leicestershire.

Bottom right: **Ransomes, Sims & Jefferies** Single-cylinder engine No 36020 was recovered from Mozambique and restored to working condition; it is seen being exhibited at Old Warden.

Burrell Single-cylinder tractor No 4083 was rebuilt from a roller, and was photographed attending a rally at Hanbury in Worcestershire.

Aveling & Porter No 1995, the fourth oldest surviving engine from this manufacturer, dating from 1884, is still up for a gentle trip around the Belvoir Castle Estate with an LMS Railway dray.

Left: **Wallis & Steevens** Expansion Engine No 7370 *Fair Rosamund*, named after the mistress of King Henry II of England, is seen here in the village of Tysoe in Warwickshire.

Above: **Marshall** General-purpose engine No 61970 from 1913 takes water at Bardwell in Suffolk.

Left: **Allchin** No 1652 *Little Mo*, built in Northampton in 1914, is supporting the NTET Driving Weekend in Worcestershire.

Right: **Aveling & Porter** Compound steam tractor No 10096 was exported to South Africa in 1921, and is seen in steam at an informal steam party in Franschoek in South Africa.

Right: **Clayton & Shuttleworth** No 36731 *Old Glory*, the mascot of a well-known monthly magazine, poses against the imposing background of Belvoir Castle in Leicestershire.

Left: **Fowler** B5 crane engine No 9403 is hauling a suitable heavy load on one of the many dirt roads on the Sandstone Estates in South Africa.

Right: **Burrell** No 3443 *Lord Nelson* spent many years as a Showman's Road Locomotive before being converted back to the form of a handsome road locomotive.

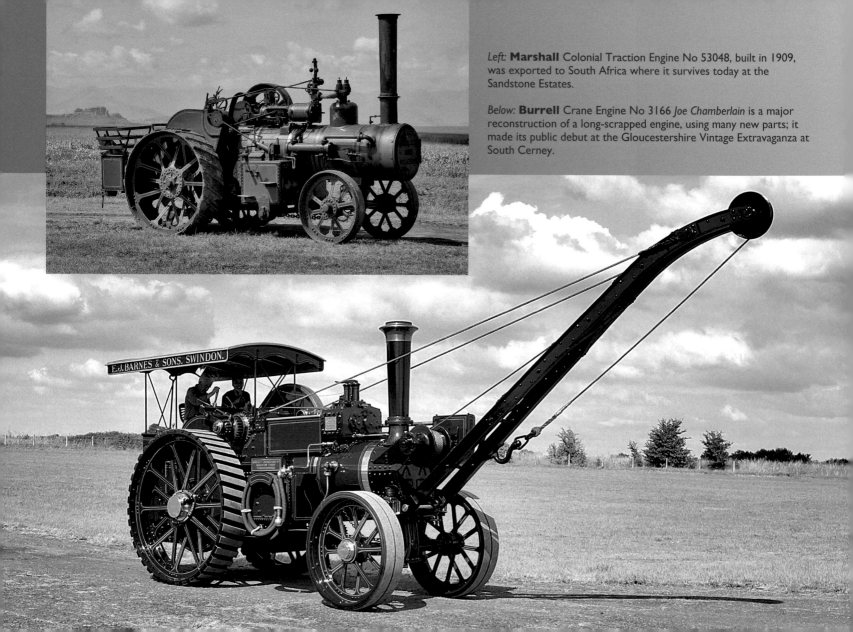

Left: **Marshall** Colonial Traction Engine No 53048, built in 1909, was exported to South Africa where it survives today at the Sandstone Estates.

Below: **Burrell** Crane Engine No 3166 *Joe Chamberlain* is a major reconstruction of a long-scrapped engine, using many new parts; it made its public debut at the Gloucestershire Vintage Extravaganza at South Cerney.

Foden Traction engine No 1310, built in 1903, was exported to Tasmania, but is now repatriated and fully restored.

Right: **McLaren** Road Locomotive No 897, built in 1905, is a tandem compound engine that spent its working life in Argentina.

Below: **Ruston & Hornsby** No 115100, built in 1920, stands in a tranquil corner of the Hartington Moor Showground.

Below right: **Ruston Proctor** Traction engine No 35829 was supplied new to a dealer in France, and remained there for many years before moving to the Netherlands, where it was restored.

Heavy haulage A demonstration at the Great Dorset Steam Fair.

Fowler Single-cylinder ploughing engine No 1642 is one of the earliest surviving examples, built in 1871.

Howard No 110 *The Farmers Friend* is a unique ploughing engine built by J. & F. Howard in Bedford. It is unusual in having the winching drum mounted horizontally across the rear of the engine.

Right: **Fowler** Compound ploughing engine No 15163 is a 'BB1' Class engine, the most numerous of preserved ploughing engines.

Below: **Fowler** The Z7 was the largest of the ploughing engines built by Fowler. This example worked on the Sena Sugar Estates in Mozambique before returning to the UK and being restored to working order.

McLaren Ploughing engine No 1552, built in 1919, is one of only two surviving examples.

Fowler Showman's Road Locomotive No 15657 was originally named *Kitchener*, but the name was changed in 1963 to *The Iron Maiden* after its starring role in the film of the same name.

Burrell 8nhp Showman's engine No 3444 *His Lordship*, built in 1913, was photographed at Belvoir Castle.

Fowler Showman's Road Locomotive No 15375 *Supremacy* was built in 1919 and is seen here in the condition that it finished its working life.

Garrett 4CD Showman's tractor No 33305 *The Mighty Atom* was built in 1918.

Burrell No 3894 *St Brannock*, rebuilt from a traction engine, heads an impressive line-up of Showman's engines at Upton-on-Severn.

Burrell No 2876, a Showman's tractor, is not equipped with a dynamo and would have been used solely for moving fairground equipment.

Garrett 4CD Showman's tractor No 33091 *Margaret*, built in 1918, passes through the village of Eastnor in Herefordshire.

Fowler Showman's engine No 20223 *Supreme* was for a short time converted to a road locomotive, as seen here at Fawley Hill.

Burrell No 4000 *Ex-Mayor*, built in 1925 and turned out unusually in blue livery, is on the road through Gamlingay in Cambridgeshire.

Burrell Showman's tractor No 3413 *The Philadelphia* complements the glorious autumn colours while on the road near Hungerford.

Foden No 2104 *Prospector* was built in 1910 and is the only survivor of the ten Showman's Road Locomotives built by Foden in Sandbach.

Burrell No 3949 *Princess Mary* is seen in the traditional setting of Carter's Steam Fair at Pinkneys Green, Berkshire.

Burrell Showman's engine No 3890 *Majestic*, built in 1922, generates after dark at the Great Dorset Steam Fair.

Left: **Fowler**
Sunny Boy No 2, Showman's engine No 10318, was built in 1905 and, after spending some years in the British Commercial Vehicle Museum at Leyland, is seen at night at the Great Dorset Steam Fair.

Right: **Foster**
Showman's tractor No 14205 *Obsession* adds to the atmosphere of the Great Dorset Steam Fair fairground.

Foden Tipper No 7768, built in 1917 as a tractor, was converted into a wagon by the War Department for use in France.

Sentinel always referred to its products as 'waggons'; this is standard waggon No 3976, built in 1921 and seen at Bishops Castle.

Foden Tractor No 12770, built in 1927, was cut down into tractor form in the 1930s and is seen here at Sambourne in Warwickshire.

Above: **Fowler** No 19708 was built as a gulley cleaner in 1931, then rebuilt from an assortment of scrap parts into a flatbed wagon.

Above right: **Sentinel** Standard No 1465 was built in about 1940 but given the identity of an older waggon; it is seen climbing the hill from Porthtowan.

Right: **Mann** These three variations of Mann's Patent Steam Cart & Wagon Co products are, from left to right, wagon No 1120 built in 1916, wagon No 1365 built in 1919, and tractor No 1386, also built in 1919.

Foden Wagon No 10320 was built in 1920, and was photographed in the courtyard of Eastnor Castle.

Garrett Overtype wagon No 34932, built in 1926, is seen at the Great Dorset Steam Fair.

Above left: **Foden** 6-ton wagon No 13178 was built in 1929, and here attends a rally in Hanbury, Worcestershire.

Above: **Sentinel** Super Two-Speed Tractor No 6426 was built in 1926 and exported to Australia, driving an ore crusher in a gold mine. It returned to the UK in 2006 and was fully restored.

Left: **Yorkshire** Wagon No 2108 was built in 1927 as a chain-driven wagon, but was later converted to shaft drive. Unusually the boiler is transversely mounted and has a central firebox and smokebox.

Above: **Sentinel** DG6 three-way tipper waggon No 8351, built in 1930, spent its working life in Scotland.

Left: **Foden** No 4258 was built as a wagon in 1914, but was restored from derelict condition as a bus.

Right: **Foden** Six-wheel tractor No 13008, built in 1928, stands at the Old Warden rally.

Left: **Sentinel** waggons were exported worldwide, and S4 Type No 9178 is preserved at the Sandstone Estates in South Africa.

Above: **Foden** 'C' Type 6-ton wagon No 13316 was originally built as a tar sprayer, but has since been modified to accept a bulk liquid tank.

Index of manufacturers

Further reading

Road Transport Recollections - Road Rollers		
ISBN 978 1 85794 553 9	Softcover	£6.00

Farming & Recollections - Steam in Agriculture		
ISBN 978 1 85794 554 6	Softcover	£6.00